Life in the Early Islamic World

Government and Law

in the Early Islamic World

Trudee Romanek

Crabtree Publishing Company

www.crabtreebooks.com

Life in the Early Islamic World

Author: Trudee Romanek
Publishing plan research and development:
   Sean Charlebois, Reagan Miller
   Crabtree Publishing Company
Editor-in-Chief: Lionel Bender
Editors: Simon Adams, Lynn Peppas
Proofreaders: Laura Booth, Wendy Scavuzzo
Editorial director: Kathy Middleton
Design and photo research: Ben White
Cover design: Katherine Berti
Production: Kim Richardson
Prepress technician: Katherine Berti
Print and production coordinator: Katherine Berti
Maps: Stefan Chabluk

Consultants:
   Barbara Petzen, Founder, Middle East Connections
   and President, Middle East Outreach Council.

Cover: Book on Islamic law, traditions, and Muslim
   obligations (top); John Sigismund of Hungary with
   Suleiman the Magnificient in 1556 (bottom right);
   Abû Zayd pleads before the Qadi of Ma'arra (bottom left)
Title page: Lahore Fort in the Punjab, Pakistan, a symbol of
   Mughal power

This book was produced for Crabtree Publishing
Company by Bender Richardson White.

Photographs and reproductions:
cover: Smithsonian Unrestricted Trust Funds, Smithsonian
   Collections Acquisition Program, & Dr. Arthur M. Sackler/
   The Bridgeman Art Library: cover (top); Wikimedia
   Commons: Les Collections de l'Histoire Les Turcs, October
   2009: cover (bottom right); The Yorck Project: 10.000
   Meisterwerke der Malerei. Distributed by DIRECTMEDIA
   Publishing GmbH.: cover (bottom left)
interior: The Art Archive: 4 (Turkish and Islamic Art Museum
   Istanbul/Collection Dagli Orti), 9 (Bibliothèque des Arts
   Décoratifs Paris/Gianni Dagli Orti), 11 (Topkapi Museum
   Istanbul/Harper Collins Publishers), 15 (Ashmolean
   Museum), 17 (Hazem Palace Damascus/Gianni Dagli Orti),
   18–19 (Collection Dagli Orti), 19 (Museum of Islamic Art
   Cairo/ Gianni Dagli Orti), 25 (National Library Cairo/Gianni
   Dagli Orti), 27 (British Library), 30–31 (Pharaonic Village
   Cairo/ Gianni Dagli Orti), 31 (Turkish and Islamic Art
   Museum Istanbul/Collection Dagli Orti), 32 (Museo Correr
   Venice/ Gianni Dagli Orti), 35 (British Library), 37 (Topkapi
   Museum Istanbul/Gianni Dagli Orti), 42 (Turkish and Islamic
   Art Museum Istanbul/Collection Dagli Orti). iStockphoto: 3
   (Egypix). shutterstock.com: 1 (Naiyyer), 4 (Ahmad Faizal
   Yahya), 6 (Dolgin Alexander Klimentyevich), 8–9 (Evgeny
   Murtola), 12 (Gyuszkofoto), 16–17 (Lizette Potgieter), 28
   (Bernhard Richter), 29 (Marc C. Johnson), 33 (Giovanni De Caro),
   34 (Serhat Akavci), 36 (Luciano Mortula), 39 (Lian Deng). Topfoto
   (The Granger Collection): 20, 23, 24; 12–13 (National Pictures),
   14 (ullsteinbild), 26, 38 (ullsteinbild), 40–41 (The Image Works)

Library and Archives Canada Cataloguing in Publication

Romanek, Trudee
   Government and law in the early Islamic world / Trudee
Romanek.

(Life in the early Islamic world)
Includes index.
Issued also in electronic formats.
ISBN 978-0-7787-2168-0 (bound).--ISBN 978-0-7787-2175-8 (pbk.)

   1. Islamic countries--Politics and government--Juvenile literature.
2. Islamic law--Juvenile literature. 3. Islamic countries--History--
Juvenile literature. I. Title. II. Series: Life in the early Islamic world

DS63.18.R65 2013   j909'.09767   C2012-907295-8

Library of Congress Cataloging-in-Publication Data

Romanek, Trudee.
 Government and law in the early Islamic world / Trudee Romanek.
   p. cm. -- (Life in the early Islamic world)
 Includes index.
 ISBN 978-0-7787-2168-0 (reinforced library binding : alk. paper) --
ISBN 978-0-7787-2175-8 (pbk. : alk. paper) -- ISBN 978-1-4271-9839-6
(electronic pdf) -- ISBN 978-1-4271-9561-6 (electronic html)
 1. Islamic countries--Politics and government--Juvenile literature. 2.
Islamic law--Juvenile literature. 3. Islamic countries--History--Juvenile
literature. 4. Islam--History--Juvenile literature. I. Title.

DS63.18.R65 2013
320.917'67--dc23
                                    2012043535

Crabtree Publishing Company

www.crabtreebooks.com   1-800-387-7650

Printed in Hong Kong/012013/BK20121102

Published in Canada
Crabtree Publishing
616 Welland Ave.
St. Catharines, Ontario
L2M 5V6

Published in the United States
Crabtree Publishing
PMB 59051
350 Fifth Avenue, 59th Floor
New York, New York 10118

Published in the United Kingdom
Crabtree Publishing
Maritime House
Basin Road North, Hove
BN41 1WR

Published in Australia
Crabtree Publishing
3 Charles Street
Coburg North
VIC, 3058

Contents

About This Book

Islam is the religion of Muslim people. Muslims believe in one God. They believe that the prophet Muhammad is the messenger of God. Islam began in the early 600s C.E. in the Arabian Peninsula, in a region that is now the country of Saudi Arabia. From there, it spread across the world. Today, there are about 1.5 billion Muslims. About half of all Muslims live in southern Asia. Many Muslims also live in the Middle East and Africa, with fewer in Europe, North America, and Australia.

The Early Islamic World—Government and Law looks at how a succession of Muslim leaders created systems of organizing, controlling, and managing their peoples from the 600s C.E. up to about 1800. It shows how their work influenced the government, laws, and structures of Muslim countries and societies today.

In the Beginning

The Bedouins were Arabs living as nomads in the desert or settled in the cities of the Arabian Peninsula. Bedouin groups constantly fought one another. Then in 610 C.E., a Bedouin Arab named Muhammad began to receive messages he said were from Allah, or God. In time, Muhammad brought the people together, became their leader, and formed a new type of Muslim government.

Below: This painting from the 1800s shows the Kaaba in Mecca, in present-day Saudi Arabia.

Above: Millions of followers of Islam journey to the *Kaaba* each year. They walk around the square, black shrine seven times as part of their worship. The Kaaba is surrounded by the world's largest **mosque**, the Al-Masjid al-Haram.

Tribes

The large peninsula of land in southwest Asia is known as Arabia. Its people, the Arabs, spoke a common language called Arabic. The main social unit among the Bedouin Arabs was the large family group called a tribe. There were certain Arab customs about how tribes and their members should behave. Members within a tribe were to get along and share their wealth with poorer members. Tribes were to be loyal **allies** to tribes of related people. They would defend and protect them against other tribes who were not related. Unrelated tribes often fought over scarce food and water in such a dry land.

Mecca

All the tribes in Arabia shared a sacred place in Mecca called the Kaaba. Each tribe placed idols of the gods they worshiped in the Kaaba. People came on pilgrimage, or religious journey, each year to pray to their gods. No weapons were allowed there, so people could worship in peace. They were not afraid of attacks by other tribes, and could trade as well.

Muhammad, the Prophet

Each Bedouin tribe had one or more gods of its own, but most recognized Allah among them. Muhammad was a religious man of the Quraysh tribe in Mecca. He was concerned that many Arabs were not caring for their poorer relatives. In 610, Muhammad began to hear messages he believed were from Allah. The messages told the Bedouins how to live. He began preaching these messages as a new religion—**Islam**. People began to follow him as a **prophet**, or messenger of God. These new followers were known as **Muslims**.

Dynasties Timeline

570 Muhammad born in Mecca
610 Muhammad tells people of his first message
622 Muhammad's followers leave Mecca for Yathrib (later called Medina)
630 Muhammad returns to Mecca
632 Muhammad dies
632–661 Rule of the first four **caliphs**
638 Muslim armies capture Jerusalem
661–750 Umayyad **caliphate**
750–1258 Abbasid caliphate
909–1171 Fatimids rule North Africa and Syria
1050 Islamic Empire expands into sub-Saharan Africa
1055 Seljuk Turkish leader seizes control of Baghdad
1143 *Quran* is translated into Latin
1171–1250 Ayyubid caliphate
1193 Islamic rule in Delhi, India
1258–1324 Osman I establishes the Ottoman state in Anatolia
1453 Mehmed II conquers Constantinople and ends Byzantine Empire
1632–1654 Taj Mahal built in India
1918 Ottomans are defeated at end of World War I
1924 The last remaining caliphate, in Turkey, is abolished

Changes

The messages Muhammad received and preached about were called the **Quran**, an Arabic word meaning **recitation**, or telling from memory. The early messages told Arabs to behave as one community and share what they have. Muhammad heard messages for 22 years. These messages also passed on other life instructions to his followers.

Islam spread throughout the Arabian Peninsula and beyond. Muhammad and the messages he shared changed the way of life for the Bedouin nomads. Before, there had been very little structure in their community. As Islam spread, the Arab way of life slowly gained new leaders and new levels of government.

The Law

For many years Arab people had followed basic laws or traditions. Tribe members, for example, protected and cared for members of their own tribe. Tribes were expected to give help, support, food, and water to travelers passing through the desert.

The Quran said that all Muslims were now like one single tribe, who should protect one another and follow new rules. These rules became the basis for more complex laws as Islam grew. By 1000, Muslims had spread from the Arabian Peninsula as far as Spain and Central Asia. As they settled in distant lands, they spread the new religious laws to the societies they found there.

Islam Grows

By the 600s, the Byzantine Empire and the Persian Empire were weak. Islam, however, was growing fast. Muslim armies spread quickly to the west as far as Spain and to the east to Central Asia. Muslim missionaries continued to spread the faith even farther, as far as China.

Right: Some Arabs still live as nomads, moving with their animals in search of new sources of food and water.

Heartland of the Empire

This map shows how the early Islamic Empire had begun in the towns of Mecca and Medina in 622 C.E., and then spread quickly across the rest of Arabia to Europe by about 750. The Byzantine Empire, based in Constantinople, ruled most of the Mediterranean lands in Muhammad's time. The Sasanians ruled what are now Iran and Iraq from their capital, Ctesiphon (near Baghdad).

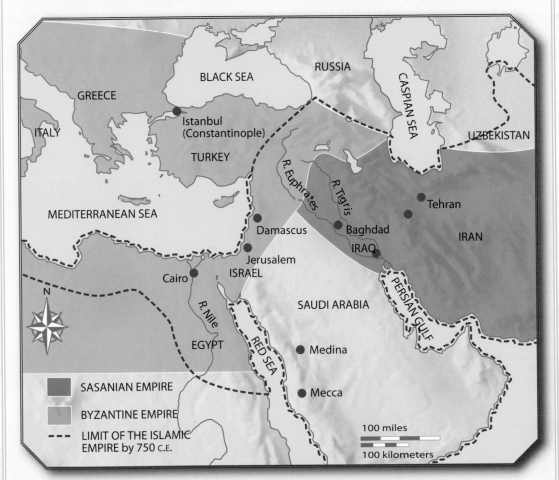

SASANIAN EMPIRE

BYZANTINE EMPIRE

- - - LIMIT OF THE ISLAMIC EMPIRE by 750 C.E.

100 miles

100 kilometers

After 750, Muslim armies then took Islam to many distant lands. Parts of the Byzantine Empire in Western Asia and North Africa were conquered, along with the Sasanian or Persian Empire to the east. Both these ancient empires were later overthrown by Muslim armies but only after many major battles and wars.

Tribal Life

Some people in pre-Islamic Arabia lived in towns and cities. These were at the edge of the desert or in oases along the trade routes where there was more water. Nomads lived in the desert, moving from one source of water to the next. Life was different for these two groups. Still, they followed many of the same traditions and had many of the same beliefs.

Below: A small **caravan**—a group of travelers—arrives at an oasis, marked by a cluster of palm trees.

Power Struggles

The Arab people were not all considered equal. Certain Arab tribes thought they were more important than others because of who their ancestors were or the wealth they had. Many tribal wars were fought and certain tribes ruled in certain areas. Small tribes often joined powerful ones, making them even more powerful. No tribe had ever grown powerful enough to control all of Arabia, however.

Unwritten Rules

Specific traditions determined how Arab people treated one another. Feuds between tribes led to injury, revenge, and more trouble. People stopped their tribe members from fighting with other tribes. In this way, the tribes controlled, or policed, their own members.

There were also traditions about revenge. Each man had a protector or someone who would avenge him if he were harmed. This tradition kept people safe. A man was less likely to attack someone if he knew that person's avenger would come after him. These and other traditions were what the early Arab people considered their rules or laws.

Water

Water was precious in the huge Arabian deserts. The Bedouins needed water for their camels and goat herds, as well as for themselves. When it was time to move on, the people loaded their belongings onto camels. They walked for days through the desert to the next oasis, or water source. The line of people and animals traveling through the desert was called a caravan.

Disagreement

Not all disputes were settled by violence. The oldest and wisest of the tribe or tribes, known as the **elders**, settled most disagreements. These men had the most experience of everyday life. They had earned the respect of the other tribe members. Their decisions were usually honored.

Below: This illustration from about 1800 shows a group of travelers resting at an oasis. It is based on a scene by the Muslim poet al-Hariri, who wrote in the 1100s.

9

The Trusted One

Muhammad was an intelligent and caring man. He was determined to help his people and make their lives better. The revelations, or sacred truths, he experienced showed him clearly how the people of his world needed to change.

Muhammad's Life

People recognized that Muhammad was trustworthy. They often asked him to help resolve their arguments. When he was a teenager, his tribe fought a battle for years with a rival tribe. Muhammad had watched his uncle help negotiate an alliance or agreement between the two tribes to end the fighting.

Over his lifetime, Muhammad came up with many solutions to people's disputes and problems. His solutions usually helped people feel equal. He became known as *al-Amin*, or "the trusted one."

Revelations

Muhammad lived in Mecca. He would often go to the nearby mountain caves to think and pray. In the year 610, while in a cave, Muhammad had what he described as a visit from Jibril, or Gabriel, a messenger from Allah. Jibril taught Muhammad that Allah was the one true God. Over the years, Muhammad had many more visions and began preaching to the Arab people about how Allah wanted them to lead their lives.

Changes

The message Muhammad passed along focused on social justice—the wealthy should not be so much richer than the poor. He spoke of forming one *umma*, or community of believers, even though the people belonged to different tribes. Muhammad wrote the first constitution, or set of laws, for the community.

Stone of the Kaaba

The Kaaba in Mecca contains an ancient black stone that Arabs believe was sent from heaven. Once, the Kaaba had to be repaired after a flood destroyed it. The elders could not decide who should replace the black stone. Muhammad suggested they place the stone on a cloth. He said four tribal elders could carry the cloth to the Kaaba, each holding one corner. In that way, no one elder was more important than the others.

Right: Muslims respect Muhammad as Islam's prophet, so many believe his face should not be shown. This 1380 picture from a story of his life shows him at the Kaaba, face covered.

واردی یدی کره کعبه طواف قلدی دخی خدجه خاتوننك

A Single Leader

To the Arab people, Muhammad was a prophet. Once his teachings were accepted by most Arabs, he became their spiritual leader. The message he brought was about being one community, so he became their social leader, too. He was a strong advisor, and he brought new rules that he insisted people follow. That made him their political leader as well.

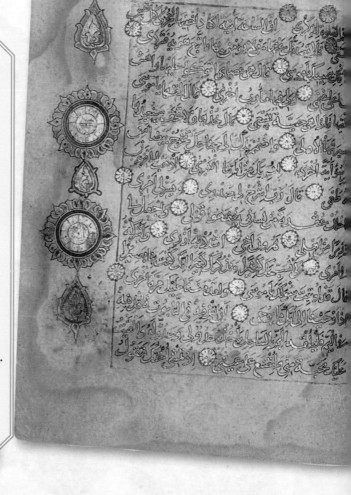

The Quran

Many of Muhammad's followers memorized the verses he recited. Muslim leaders after Muhammad asked **scribes** to write down in the Quran all the verses revealed to Muhammad. The stories Muhammad told and other lessons he taught were also carefully recorded. These were called the *hadiths*, or recollections. Together, these writings form the sacred texts of Islam. Over the centuries, many scholars have studied and memorized both the Quran and the hadiths.

Below: Modern printed editions of the Quran, which has 114 *suras* or chapters.

Muhammad's Legacy

Slowly, Muhammad built a new community, a new religion, and a new social order. At the core of these was a set of rituals, beliefs, and laws that governed how Muslims should live together. These clear guidelines paved the way for setting up systems of justice throughout the Islamic Empire.

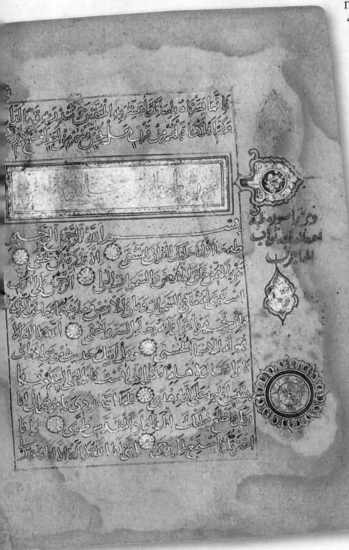

After the Prophet

Muhammad died in 632 C.E. As a prophet, he could not be replaced. But the Muslims needed a new political leader. Most Muslims believe that Muhammad did not appoint anyone to follow him as leader. There were no clear rules as to who should come after him. Everyone had trouble agreeing on who should be the new leader, or **caliph**. Caliph means "successor," or the one who comes next. The umma finally chose a new leader from among Muhammad's most loyal followers. They appointed his good friend Abu Bakr as their political and military leader. In the two years he served as caliph, Abu Bakr gained control over all Arabia.

Succession Troubles

Arguments continued about who should be the next leader. Abu Bakr chose as his successor a man named Umar ibn al-Khattab. Umar was killed in his tenth year as caliph. Muslim elders decided his successor would be Uthman ibn Affan. Then Uthman was also killed in 656. Ali ibn Abi Talib was Muhammad's cousin and son-in-law. He became the fourth caliph. Not all Muslims were happy with him as leader, though.

Left: This early Quran is dated 1203 and is written in ornate Arabic lettering with gold and silver decorations.

Early Government

Before Islam, Arab tribal chiefs ruled small numbers of people with one language and a shared way of life. Now, the growing Muslim umma was much larger, with many more people of different backgrounds. The early caliphs needed to understand and rule this enormous new empire. They appointed governors in each region to look after its needs.

The Divide

A rift formed in Islam over who should become the rightful leader of the umma. One group felt only those who were related to Muhammad by blood should succeed him as leader. That group is now known as the **Shii** Muslims. They supported Ali ibn Abi Talib, the fourth caliph, but not the first three. **Sunni** Muslims did not feel a blood relationship was required. They believed the first three caliphs were valid caliphs. These two Muslim groups—Shii and Sunni—exist to this day.

Left: This artwork of Muhammad appointing his cousin Ali ibn Abi Talib as his successor supports the Shii viewpoint of who should rightfully lead the Muslim people.

First Caliphs

Abu Bakr was caliph for two years. After him, Umar expanded the Islamic Empire beyond the Arabian Peninsula. He sent armies to battle the nearby Byzantine and Sasanian empires. His armies captured new lands in Syria, Persia, Egypt, and across North Africa.

Umar then had to oversee all these lands. Other rulers often gave pieces of the new territory to the soldiers who had conquered it. Umar did not. He considered the land to be owned by the umma. He paid soldiers to live there and settled them in camp cities, ready to fight against any enemies. As he lay dying, Umar formed a **council** of six men to choose the new caliph.

Uthman ibn Affan served as the third caliph after Muhammad's death. Many historians say he was the caliph who had scribes collect and write down all of the revelations of Muhammad as the Quran. Some believe he governed poorly.

Ali ibn Abi Talib, the fourth caliph, was leader of his people for only five years. In that time, most of his efforts were spent trying to resolve **civil wars** within the Islamic world.

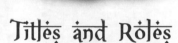

Below: This gold coin shows Abd al-Malik ibn Marwan, caliph in the late 600s.

Titles and Roles

Under the early caliphs, there were other leaders. Governors were the political rulers in each province. Military leaders of the armies were called *emirs*, or commanders. Religious leaders were called the *ulema*, or learned ones. A member of the ulema could serve as an *imam*, or prayer leader. For Shii Muslims, the imam was the rightful spiritual and political leader of the umma, descended from the prophet's family line.

Early Dynasties

Muawiyah of the Umayyad clan, who was the governor of Syria, rose up against Caliph Ali. After Ali died in 661, Muawiyah became the first caliph of the Umayyad dynasty, **or family of rulers. The Umayyads were later overthrown by the Abbasids, who founded their own dynasty in 750.**

The Umayyad Dynasty

The Umayyad dynasty, with its capital Damascus, established a new tradition of passing down the caliphate within their own family. Under their rule, the Islamic Empire expanded east toward India and China and west across North Africa to Spain, which they called al-Andalus.

The Umayyads established a postal service to communicate across this vast area. One of the most successful rulers of the Umayyad dynasty was Abd al-Malik ibn Marwan. He created new coins and made Arabic the official language of the empire.

The Abbasid Dynasty

In 750, a new group of Muslims called the Abbasids seized power. In Iraq, the Abbasid caliph al-Mansur built a new capital called Baghdad. Meanwhile, the last remaining member of the Umayyad family had fled to al-Andalus and set up a rival caliphate there. The Abbasids

The Vizier

The new position of **vizier**, or chief advisor, developed in the Abbasid government. A lowly person, even a slave, could become vizier and rise in importance. Over time, a shift took place. The viziers, their officials, and military leaders became more powerful while the caliphs they had advised and worked for became less important.

Right: In 691, Umayyad caliph Abd al-Malik completed the Dome of the Rock shrine in Jerusalem.

encouraged trade, and the amount of goods imported and exported grew. The empire grew wealthy.

Perhaps the most famous Abbasid caliph was Harun al-Rashid. In his time, the empire had a cultural boom. Scientists, scholars, and artists came to Baghdad and made enormous advances in medicine, astronomy, physics, philosophy, literature, law, and many other fields. Even in that time of riches and learning, however, there was still war. Power struggles and civil wars were expensive and weakened the empire, which began to splinter into different pieces.

Above: Caliph al-Walid, another Umayyad ruler and son of Abd al-Malik, built the famous Great Mosque in Damascus, Syria, in the early 700s.

The Challengers

The Abbasid dynasty served as caliphs until 1258. In the later years, they were not the all-powerful rulers they had once been. Other groups, including the Fatimids, Buyids, and Seljuks, divided their empire. They took control in various regions. This left the Abbasid caliph with authority only in religious matters.

Fatimids

The Fatimids were a dynasty of Shii Muslims in North Africa. Their leaders were descended from the prophet Muhammad's daughter Fatima and her husband Ali ibn Abi Talib, Muhammad's cousin and the fourth caliph. They opposed Abbasid Sunni rule and said that they, not the Abbasids, were the rightful leaders of the Muslims.

The Fatimid imam Ubayd Allah al-Mahdi declared himself caliph in 909 in Tunisia. By 1000, the Fatimids had conquered Egypt and part of Syria. They built the new city of Cairo as their capital. They also founded the university of al-Azhar and a great library.

Right: In 1176, the Seljuks conquered the Turkish city of Eskişehir, shown in this artwork by the artist Matrakçi Nasuh.

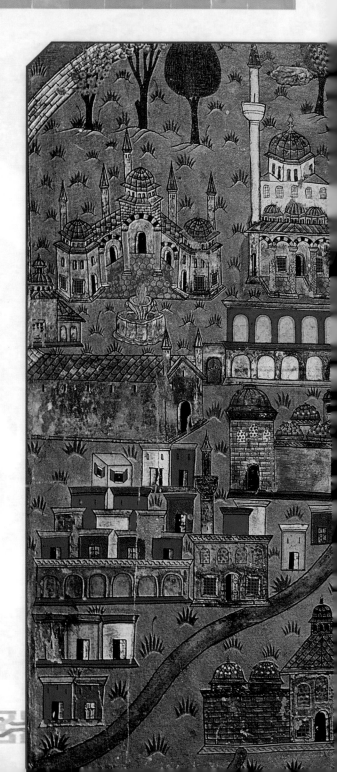

Left: This portrait is part of a larger work of art from the time of Fatimid rule in Egypt.

Ghilman

The Abbasid rulers needed to add more soldiers to their armies to remain strong. Caliph al-Mu'tasim brought in new soldiers from their eastern borders. Many of these men were Turkish slaves or prisoners of war captured during earlier conquests. These new soldiers were known as **ghilmans**. Their job was to protect the caliph. Eventually, these soldiers became more powerful and they could decide who would become the next caliph.

Buyids

The Buyids were another group of Shii Muslims who were becoming powerful in the east. In 945, these tribesmen took control of the Abbasid capital of Baghdad. Their leader was Ali ibn Buya. Ali called himself the "Great Commander." He did not overthrow the caliph. Instead he insisted that the Abbasids let his group rule several areas as separate states. The Buyids claimed to be under the control of the Abbasids. They behaved, however, as though they were kings of their own lands.

Seljuks

Seljuk ibn Duqaq was the leader of a group of Turkish tribesmen from Central Asia. In the late 900s, these tribesmen began moving toward the Middle East. They found that the Islamic Empire was now divided into several weaker states.

The Seljuks conquered much of Persia. In 1055, one of their leaders, Togrul Beg, captured Baghdad. The Abbasid caliph lost his official powers, and he gave Togrul the title of **sultan**, or military leader, of the East and West. The Seljuks held power throughout most of the 1100s in Baghdad, and up to about 1300 in Anatolia (today's Turkey).

Sharia Law

The verses of the Quran outline how faithful Muslims should live their lives. The instructions people are to follow are known as the *Sharia*, an Arabic word that means "road" or "path." These religious guidelines formed the basis of the laws that governed life for Muslims throughout the Early Islamic Empire.

Rules for Living

The Quran provided the most important guidance for Muslims in the early Islamic Empire. It told them to take good care of everything, from Earth to their fellow Muslims. It advised people to be kind and fair and to avoid doing wrong. Early Muslims applied these basic principles, or rules of good behavior, as well as others from the Quran. These principles helped them judge between right and wrong actions. They helped them devise laws to be followed in many aspects of their lives.

Muslims believe that any action a person takes falls into one of five categories: actions that are required, recommended, allowed, discouraged, or forbidden. Required actions include such things as daily prayers. They are actions that must be done. Actions that are simply allowed are considered neither good nor bad. Forbidden actions are things that a Muslim should never do. Stealing something is an example of a forbidden action.

Sharia also considers a person's intentions. Whether someone intended to do a good deed or a bad one is important.

The Hadiths

The *hadiths* are the stories about what Muhammad said and did during his lifetime. His followers wrote down all these stories, just as they recorded the verses of the Quran. Muhammad's example was a model of how to live a good life as a Muslim, how to treat others, and how to worship God.

Day of Judgement

The Quran says that there will be a day when God will judge all people according to their actions. Muslims believe that those who have followed the guidelines of the Quran will pass to a never-ending afterlife in a wonderful paradise. Those whose actions have been bad rather than good will spend their afterlife in a place of endless punishment called hell.

Above: Many Islamic stories and paintings describe the paradise of those who had lived what the Quran said was a life of goodness. Others showed the eternal life of those who were bad. This illustration from the 1400s shows Muhammad visiting the part of hell where people who stole money from orphans lie amid flames, while demons pour poison into their mouths.

The Study of Fiqh

As more people converted to Islam, it became important to have a reliable way to decide on the laws that good Muslims were to follow. Scholars studied the Quran and hadiths. They decided how to interpret their meanings and guidance in new or more complicated situations. This study was called **Fiqh**, meaning "deep understanding." The Fiqh formed, and still forms, the basis of legal decision and punishments in some Muslim countries.

Major Schools of Fiqh

There have been many interpretations of law since the first years of Islam. Some of

Above: These Muslim boys in Afghanistan are reading the Quran in order to understand its message and teachings.

the earliest interpretations still influence Islamic law today. The legal systems of countries such as Iraq, Sudan, Egypt, and Saudi Arabia are all based primarily on the interpretations of five main schools, known as the Hanafi, Maliki, Shafii, Hanbali, and Jafari schools. Islamic legal scholars founded all five schools in the 600s to 800s.

The differences between these schools were in most cases minor. All of them agreed on the basic principles of Islam.

Legal Titles

In Muslim societies, the ulema filled several important roles. A scholar of Fiqh was called a *faqih* and would often teach students about Islamic law in a university or *madrasa*. A **mufti** was a respected scholar who could be asked to give a **fatwa**, or legal opinion, on a matter under consideration. A **qadi**, or judge, was appointed by the ruler to decide disputes between people or sentence criminals.

Female Scholars

Although most scholars were men, there were some women. In the 800s, Ayesha bint Yusuf al-Baniyah from Damascus was granted a license to be a teacher of law as well as a mufti.

Amrah bint Abdur-Rahman was a hadith scholar and a mufti. Umm al-Darda and Fatima bint Ibrahim ibn Jowhar were both considered great teachers who taught some of the most respected scholars.

Above: Marriage is considered a legal contract in Islam. In this illustration, the Indian Muslim emperor Shah Jahan is shown riding to the wedding of his son, Dara Shikoh.

Muslim Women

Early Muslim men and women were considered equal as believers but had different roles and rights in society. For example, early Muslim women could own land and inherit property, but their share was less than a brother's would be. They had the right to refuse a marriage, but they were expected to obey their husbands. Husbands could divorce their wives easily, but it was much more difficult for women to divorce.

Islamic Justice

The Quran describes a few actions that are criminal. These include murder and robbery. It also outlines punishments for those who commit these crimes. Over time, the Sharia developed to include information on judging and punishing many more crimes than those mentioned in the Quran.

Above: In this Muslim court, a man pleads his case to the qadi, or judge, who sits on the left.

Types of Crime

In Islamic law, crimes are divided into different groups. One group consists of crimes against a person's honor. These include telling lies about a person. Another group includes crimes that involve taking things that belong to someone else. A further group has to do with injuring another person.

Punishments

People who committed crimes were punished. Some serious crimes had a set punishment. For others, the qadi could decide what punishment was fair. The qadi considered whether each crime was an action against another person or against God. The punishment could depend on whether the crime was committed on purpose or by accident.

There were several different types of punishments such as imprisonment, whipping, and paying money to the victim or his family. A person who told lies about someone might be sentenced to 80 lashes with a whip. A thief who stole even a small item could have one or both hands cut off. Someone who robbed a traveler might be banished, or sent out of the community. A highway robber could be sentenced to die for his crime.

Most cities had prisons. Often these prisons were just used as a place to keep criminals until they were punished. People who would not pay money they owed others were sometimes sentenced to spend some time in a prison.

Above: This man has been sentenced to hang for his crimes.

Sentenced to Death

In many ancient cultures, some criminals were sentenced to death. This was true under early Islamic law for the most serious crimes such as committing murder while stealing. An executioner would carry out the sentence. He would cut off the head of the prisoner or hang him by a rope around his neck. A few criminals were killed by stoning. That meant that a group of people would throw stones at them until they died.

Scoundrels and Invaders

Every society has people who choose not to obey the laws. These people usually break the laws so they can gain money or power. A few criminal groups in the Islamic Empire defied Muslim rules. Enemies such as the Mongols ignored Muslim laws and invaded large areas of the Islamic Empire.

Assassins

In the 1100s, a group of men from Syria known as Nazari Ismailis formed a force of special fighters. These men sought out and killed the main enemies of their community. Legends suggest that these men were highly trained killers. This may not have been true. Other Muslims and Europeans sometimes called them by the Arabic word *hashashin*. The modern word "assassin" comes from this name. An assassin is a person who carries out plans to kill people.

Below: As a few scoundrels called *thuggees* get the victim to look up to expose his neck, another prepares to strangle him with a scarf. Thuggees existed in Muslim India from the 1300s to the late 1800s.

Cheats

Early Islamic law was also concerned with regulating business deals. Cheating someone in a trade was a religious and civic crime. The *muhtasib*, or market inspector, made sure that merchants were fair and accurate in all their dealings. A goldsmith could be punished for selling jewelry that was not solid gold but only coated with gold, or a baker if his loaves were under the stated weight.

Mongols

In 1206, the Mongol chieftain Temujin, or Genghis Khan, united the Mongol people of Eastern Asia under his leadership. Mongol armies raided and conquered large parts of northern China.

In 1219, the Mongols invaded the lands of the powerful Muslim ruler Khwarazm-Shah. The cities in these lands were centers of Islamic culture. The Mongols fought their way through the areas known today as Turkmenistan, northern Afghanistan, and parts of Iran. Khwarazm-Shah and his thriving cities were destroyed.

After Genghis Khan died, other Mongol leaders expanded his territory. By 1258, the Mongols controlled what is today Georgia, Armenia, and northern Azerbaijan. They also attacked Baghdad and killed the Abbasid caliph.

Right: This illustration shows Genghis Khan and his Mongol fighters battling Chinese soldiers in the mountains. By 1279, the entire Chinese Empire was in Mongol hands.

Police

As early as 660, there was a type of police force founded to stop crime and enforce the laws in cities of the Islamic Empire. This force was called the **shurta**. It worked alongside the courts of law and the qadis. Its officers worked as night watchmen, overseers of the market, enforcers of public order, bodyguards to the ruler, and protectors of the trade routes. They were also responsible for punishing criminals.

Other Communities

Most of the time, members of the Muslim communities got along well with people of other religions. At other times, there was conflict between the groups. If a particular ruler allowed non-Muslims to follow their ways, the relationship was usually good.

Below: Different religions have always fought over Jerusalem. In 1009, Caliph al-Hakim ordered the Christian Church of the Holy Sepulchre to be destroyed. The church shown below was rebuilt on the same site.

Dhimma

People of other religions often lived in lands ruled by Muslims. The Quran says that these people had to accept Muslim rule and pay a tribute of some money or part of a harvest. Once they did, Muslims were to protect them. That agreement is called *dhimma* in Islamic law.

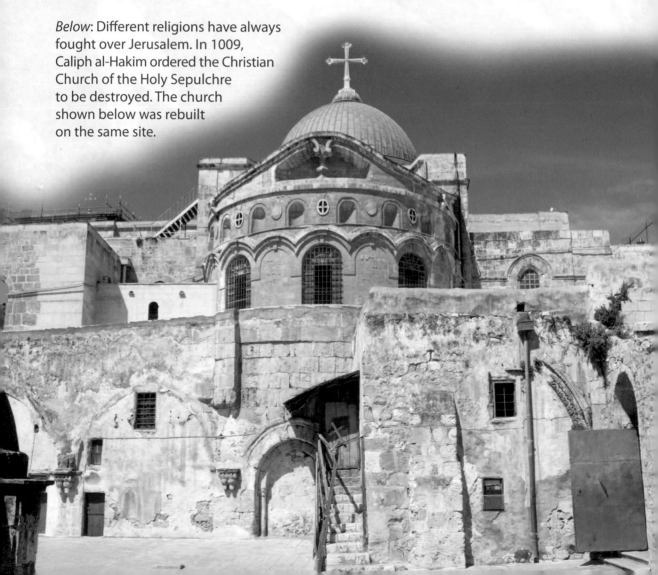

Right: Zoroastrianism was the major religion of Persia before the Muslim conquest. Its followers build special fire temples, like this one, for worship.

Umayyad Attitudes

Muhammad and his early successors had required the pagan tribes of Arabia to convert to Islam when they joined the umma, or community. The Umayyad rulers, though, had a large population of Christians, Jews, and Zoroastrians in their territory, who were useful merchants, artisans, and scholars. As the Quran stated, the Umayyads allowed these non-Muslims who worshiped one God to follow their own religion if they paid a special tax. Many non-Muslims chose to convert to Islam. Becoming a Muslim meant that they could not be made slaves. They would also have to pay less tax.

In the 700s, Caliph al-Walid destroyed the Christian church of St. John the Baptist in Damascus to build the Great Mosque. He did, however, include a shrine to St. John in the mosque.

Jerusalem

The city of Jerusalem is sacred to Jews and Christians, as well as to Muslims. Jews believed it was the city of King David and the site of the first Jewish temple. Christians believed Jesus Christ was crucified and buried there. For Muslims, Muhammad ascended to heaven from Jerusalem. Followers of all three religions wanted access to their holy sites.

Kurds and Muslims

The Kurds were a tribal people living in the western part of what is now called Turkey. They wanted to be free to choose their religion and follow their traditional ways. Some battled against the Umayyads but fought alongside the Abbasid and Seljuk armies. Some people of Kurdish origins became great leaders.

The Crusades

In 1095, the head of the Roman Catholic Church, Pope Urban II, asked the lords and knights of Europe to go fight for Christians living in Jerusalem and Constantinople under Muslim rulers. The men who responded became known as Crusaders.

Constantinople

By about 1090, the Seljuks were threatening Constantinople, capital of the Christian Eastern Roman, or Byzantine, Empire. The Byzantine emperor asked for help defending the city. Urban II called on Christians in Europe to march east. In 1096 and 1097, many arrived to defend Constantinople, but most continued on to fight in the Holy Land (important sites in the Bible). About 100 years later, a new group of Christian knights arrived. Instead of protecting Constantinople, they attacked it and stole everything of value to take back to Europe.

Jerusalem

Pope Urban II also wanted to gain control over Muslim-ruled Jerusalem. Thousands

of Crusaders fought battles as they marched down the Mediterranean coast toward Jerusalem.

Some Muslim rulers gathered armies together to fight the Crusaders. Others gave the Crusaders some land to stop the fighting. Yet others became allies with the Crusaders and fought with them against their own Muslim rivals. Some Muslims and Crusaders even formed friendships.

In 1099, the Christian Crusaders attacked Jerusalem. They killed many of the Muslims who lived there, as well as many Jews and unwelcome Christians. In 1187, the Kurdish general Salah al-Din, or Saladin, regained control of the city.

In response, King Richard I of England traveled from England to the Middle East and fought against Saladin. Richard did not recapture Jerusalem, although he did win two big battles. He and Saladin signed a peace agreement in 1192 that allowed Christian pilgrims to visit Jerusalem, which remained in Muslim hands.

Above: This Ottoman artwork shows the Muslims at the gates of Jerusalem defeating the Christians and recapturing the city.

Left: A later painting shows Saladin fighting in this same battle for Jerusalem.

Winners and Losers

Eight major and many minor Crusades set out from many countries in Europe between 1096 and 1291 to free the Christian holy places in Palestine from Muslim control. The Crusaders won several battles, but eventually lost all the territory they had originally gained.

The Ottomans

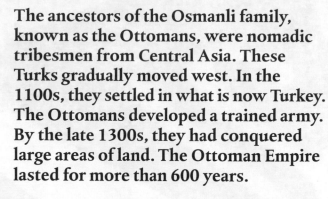

The ancestors of the Osmanli family, known as the Ottomans, were nomadic tribesmen from Central Asia. These Turks gradually moved west. In the 1100s, they settled in what is now Turkey. The Ottomans developed a trained army. By the late 1300s, they had conquered large areas of land. The Ottoman Empire lasted for more than 600 years.

Osman and His Sons

The first important leader of the Ottomans was Osman I. The name "Ottoman" comes from his name. He was leader from 1281 until his death in 1326. Osman's son Orhan

Byzantine Clerks

The Byzantine Empire came after the great Roman Empire. The Byzantines had a strong history of organized government and taxation. The new Ottoman rulers appreciated their skills. When they took over Byzantine settlements, they encouraged the clerks of the old empire to stay on. In that way, they made use of Byzantine expertise in record keeping.

Left: This Ottoman man from the 1600s was in charge of finances.

greatly expanded the new state and ruled until his death in 1360. He conquered the city of Bursa and created a great Islamic center there.

Orhan's son Murad I was next in line, ruling the Ottoman Empire until 1389. He made a more organized government and founded a new type of army (see page 34). In 1383, he took on the title of **sultan**, meaning a leader with great authority.

Life of a Sultan

A sultan was a Muslim military leader who had complete control in the region he ruled. He was considered to be in charge of upholding Sharia law but he had no

Above: The Topkapi Palace in Constantinople was the largest and grandest palace in the Ottoman Empire. This is a view of the tiled walls and ceiling.

religious authority, unlike a caliph. Sultans were the ultimate power on almost all issues other than those concerning faith. These military leaders got stronger and the caliphs lost power.

Many Ottoman sultans lived in Topkapi Palace in Constantinople. The palace had gardens, stables, kitchens, and a section called the **harem**, in which his mother, wives, children, other female relatives, slave girls, and servants all lived.

Janissary Corps

The **Janissary Corps** was a special force of soldiers established by Murad I in the late 1300s. It was made up of prisoners of war and then from young boys collected from Christian villages. Their excellent training, loyalty to the sultan, and strict discipline made them feared military fighters. The janissaries helped the Ottomans expand their empire through the 1400s and 1500s. They gained so much power, they could determine who would be the next sultan.

Timur

In the mid-1300s, a young man named Timur grew up as a member of a Mongol tribe. He was a wise man but a savage warrior. He became leader of his tribe in about 1361 and converted to Islam.

Below: The center of this mosaic shows a sultan's tughra. A tughra was a type of signature used on firmans and other documents.

He then led his army westward and won many battles against both new and old enemies. Sometimes he defeated his opponents but did not take over their land. With all of the riches he won, he founded a capital city at Samarkand. While the Ottoman Empire was growing, Timur was winning battles in Russia, South Asia, and the Middle East and sacking Delhi, Damascus, and Baghdad.

In 1402, he fought Ottoman forces near today's city of Ankara. Although he defeated its army, he did not take over as Ottoman ruler. When Timur died in 1405, the Ottomans regained power. Timur became known as Tamerlane.

Victory for Mehed II

In 1453, the Ottoman sultan Mehmed II defeated the Byzantines and captured Constantinople. Mehmed II announced that it was to be his new capital. He converted its main church into a mosque, built many palaces, and boosted trade in the city. The Ottomans had brought the Byzantine Empire to an end.

Firmans

The Ottoman rulers respected Sharia law, but realized it did not cover all aspects of life. They therefore created a legal document called a **firman**. In Persian, that means an order or a decree. A firman included a set of rules or laws outside of religious laws.

Above: In this Indian painting from 1600, Timur sits in his garden. The man kneeling before him is the Ottoman sultan.

Suleiman's Laws

After the conquest of Constantinople, the Ottoman sultans continued to expand their empire. They took over land in present-day Hungary, Romania, Iraq, Palestine, the Arabian Peninsula, Egypt, and much of North Africa. Suleiman became Ottoman sultan in 1520. He is considered one of the greatest Muslim rulers and is often called Suleiman the Magnificent.

Sharia could not always provide answers to questions of taxation, land ownership, criminal law, or trade. Suleiman needed a structured legal system that would cover these issues of state. He improved the existing system to fill this need. The people of the empire called Suleiman *Kanuni*, or Law-Giver.

The Law-Giver

Suleiman wanted his courts to uphold Sharia law. But he knew that Sharia could not deal with all the non-religious issues of his people.

Right: The Suleymaniye Mosque was built in Constantinople from 1550 to 1558. Within its buildings were a hospital, schools, and a kitchen that fed the poor.

Right: The son of the king of Hungary bows down in front of Suleiman the Magnificent on his visit to Suleiman's court in 1566.

A Well-Organized System

Suleiman's legal system was created with a few people in charge at the top and more people in power beneath them. This structure helped him better control the many regions of the empire.

Suleiman created a new type of military qadi and a new state mufti. These officials sat at the head of the system. Below them were the qadis of the cities and large towns. Serving under them were the qadis who each had authority over one small district. The qadis in this system became part of the government. They had more duties. They made sure that justice was carried out fairly and that prisoners were looked after. They also served as a link between people and government.

Legacy

The major improvements Suleiman made to the Ottoman government kept the empire strong for years. He also improved other areas of society, such as education, and supported many artists. He ordered the building of many important structures. These include the Suleymaniye Mosque in Constantinople and the Selimiye Mosque in Adrianople.

Beyond the Middle East

Above: An Indian prince rides an elephant in this painting from about 1600.

Over hundreds of years, Islam spread from the Middle East to many other areas of the world. Muslim armies won battles and gained land from Morocco and Spain in the west to India in the east. It also spread to places such as Indonesia as traders and missionaries convinced people to convert to the new religion.

The Far East

In 651, a Muslim messenger went to China. Muslim traders then brought Islam to the Chinese. When the Mongol Yuan dynasty ruled parts of China, many Muslims settled there. They served in the Mongol governments. Islam spread farther east to the islands of Indonesia. Parts of Malaya, Java, and Sumatra became important Muslim territories.

Africa

Islam quickly spread west through Egypt and along Africa's north coast. Merchants preached Islam across the Sahara Desert. Trader ships sailed down Africa's east coast, taking their faith to the ports they visited. Islam eventually spread to more than one third of Africa.

India

In 1560, Akbar the Great, a descendant of Timur, became the leader of the Mughal Empire in northern India. Akbar was respectful of the different religions of the Indian people. He funded new projects in architecture, literature, and painting. He did not force his Indian subjects to convert to Islam. By the early 1700s, Muslim rulers controlled most of India.

Above: The Id Kah Mosque is the largest mosque in China. It was originally built in 1442 and can hold 20,000 worshipers.

Islam in the World

Muslim rulers oversaw many parts of the world. Their countries all shared the religion of Islam, but they were not all governed the same. The laws and legal systems were different. In most countries, there was a major emphasis on religion and faith. Suleiman the Magnficent, for example, was very religious. The Ottoman sultans who ruled after him were not. Each empire was slightly different in its own way from its Muslim neighbors.

Modern Times

After the 1500s, the world began to change. European explorers discovered North and South America and set up new trading networks. The Ottoman Empire and other Muslim states stopped expanding and soon lost territory to a more powerful Europe. Today, Islam is the second-largest religion in the world after Christianity.

End of the Ottomans

The rise of Europe worked against the Ottomans. British and Dutch traders who had always crossed Ottoman lands to reach Asia now sailed there instead. The Ottomans missed out on much trade. The later Ottoman sultans could not keep the government and army as strong. Some Ottoman regions declared themselves **independent**, or free from the sultan's control. During World War I, from 1914 to 1918, the Ottomans were defeated. In 1923, the area became the **Republic** of Turkey. A president replaced the last Ottoman sultan.

Muslim Regions

Muslims today live in countries around the globe. Some mostly Muslim states are governed by a king. Saudi Arabia and Morocco are both ruled by kings who inherit the throne. Other countries are republics. People elect their leader in a republic. Pakistan and Turkey are both republics. The legal system in some kingdoms and republics is based on Sharia law. In others, the law is more **secular**, or non-religious.

In 2011, there were uprisings in the Muslim countries of Tunisia, Libya, and Egypt as the people there overthrew leaders they were not happy with.

Right: These children in Dearborn, Michigan, ride a roller coaster at the Arab International Festival. Dearborn is home to the largest Muslim community in the United States.

Islamic Judgments

Many Muslims believe certain things are sacred. The Western world values free speech. Sometimes this brings Muslim values and secular law into conflict. In 1988, the British author Salmon Rushdie wrote a book that some Muslims felt insulted Islam. The ruler of Iran issued a fatwa that Rushdie should be killed, and he had to go into hiding for years. In 2005, a Danish artist drew cartoons that mocked Muhammad. Muslims were outraged and felt he should be punished.

Female Leaders

While some Muslims believe only men should be political leaders, several women have been elected by their people to head Muslim countries. Benazir Bhutto was elected prime minister of Pakistan in 1988. Tansu Çiller was elected prime minister of Turkey in 1993. Indonesia elected Megawati Sukarnoputri president in 2001.

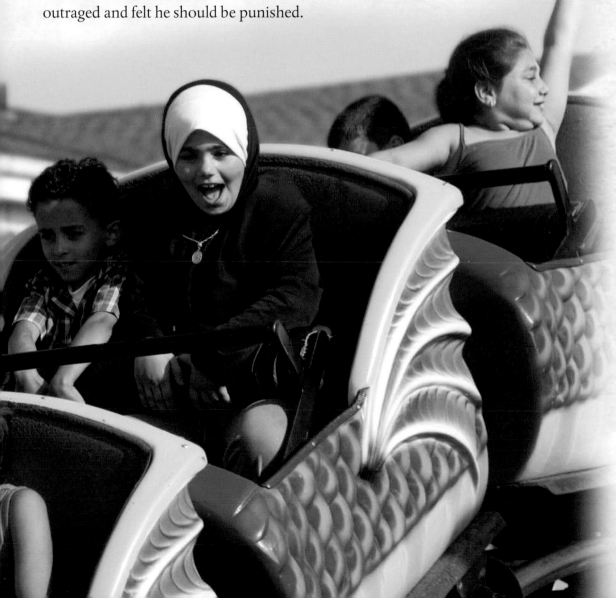

Biographies

Abu Bakr (573–634)

Abu Bakr was Muhammad's close friend and one of the first to follow his teachings. Abu Bakr was chosen Muslim caliph after Muhammad's death. He resolved many rebellions among the Muslim followers.

Umar Ibn Al-Khattab (586–644)

Before he died, Abu Bakr named Umar as the next caliph. Umar oversaw the early growth of the empire. He made decisions about the dividing up of conquered lands and the treatment of non-Muslims.

Uthman Ibn Affan (579–656)

Muslims disagree about Uthman's role in early Islam. Some accuse him of unfairly giving land and important positions to his family members. Sunni Muslims see him as one of the early honorable caliphs. Shiis believe that Ali rather than Uthman should have been the third caliph.

Ali Ibn Abi Talib (598–661)

Shii Muslims believe that Ali ibn Abi Talib was the first true caliph after Muhammad. Ali had lived in Muhammad's home since the age of five, he was a cousin, and he had married Muhammad's daughter, Fatima. While he was caliph, civil war split the new Muslim community.

Aisha Bint Abu Bakr (614–678)

Muhammad's second wife was Aisha, the daughter of Abu Bakr. Aisha and some followers rebelled against the ourth caliph, Ali, but were defeated. She was an important figure in politics and also helped preserve Muhammad's deeds and words for the umma.

Abd Al-Malik Ibn Marwan (646–705)

Abd al-Malik was a capable Umayyad caliph who strengthened the empire despite many revolts. He built the Dome of the Rock in Jerusalem.

Harun Al-Rashid (765–809)

Harun al-Rashid ruled the Abbasid Empire from 786 until 809. His court in Baghdad was a place of fabled luxury. His vizier looked after many of the affairs of government. Harun al-Rashid is the caliph famously mentioned in *The Book of One Thousand and One Nights*, although they were actually written much later.

Togrul Beg (990–1063)

Togrul Beg was an important Seljuk Turkish military leader who captured Baghdad in 1055. He was named sultan and reduced the power of the Abbasid caliphs so they were leaders in name only.

Saladin (1138–1193)

The warrior Salah al-Din Yusuf ibn Ayyub, or Saladin, was born in Iraq in about 1138. He was of Kurdish background and well educated in the Quran. At age 14, he became a soldier like his father and uncle to fight against the Crusaders. From 1170 to 1180, he was sultan of Egypt and Syria. Saladin was famous in the West for his recapture of Jerusalem from its Christian rulers in 1187 and for his rivalry with King Richard I of England.

Below: A watercolor of Sultan Suleiman the Magnificent

Genghis Khan (1162–1227)

This Mongol general is renowned for his military brilliance. His obedient army was practically unbeatable for more than 40 years. His soldiers killed and destroyed everyone and everything in their path. Once in power, however, he promoted trade and exchange across his territories.

Osman I (1258–1326)

Osman I, or Osman Gazi, was one of many tribesmen fighting for land in what is now Turkey. As leader from around 1300, he founded the Ottoman Empire that was eventually to control much of the Middle East and North Africa.

Mehmed II (1432–1481)

Sometimes called Mehmed the Conqueror, Mehmed II was a descendant of Osman I. His father made him ruler of the city of Edirne when he was just 12. He ended the Byzantine Empire by conquering Constantinople in 1453 and, as a result of more battles, expanded the Ottoman Empire into southern Europe.

Suleiman (1495–1566)

As sultan of the Ottoman Empire, Suleiman the Magnificent extended new rights to Europeans living under his rule. He negotiated a treaty that stated European traders who committed a crime in the empire would be tried according to their own laws, rather than Islamic law.

The Extent of the Early Islamic World

Early Muslim merchants, traders, and armies took their faith, customs, and learning right across the world. From the 600s on, Islam spread throughout the Arabian Peninsula into the Middle East, northern Africa, Spain, India, and Indonesia. It also reached parts of China and many other parts of Asia. This map shows areas that were under Muslim rule after the first main conquests (up to the year 750) and then at the height of the Islamic Empire. Islamic systems of government and law have had a massive influence on world history and have shaped many of the Muslim countries in the world today.

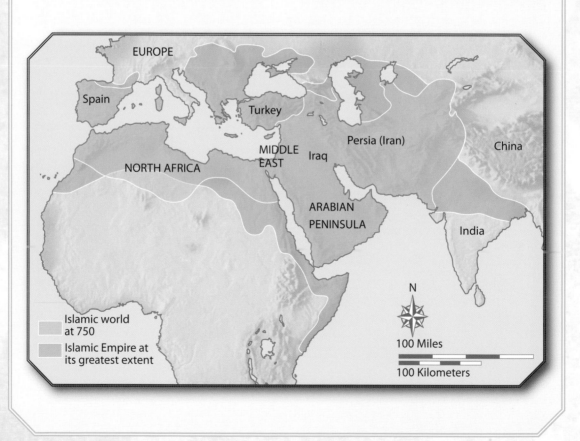

EUROPE

Spain

Turkey

Persia (Iran)

China

MIDDLE EAST

Iraq

NORTH AFRICA

ARABIAN PENINSULA

India

N

Islamic world at 750

Islamic Empire at its greatest extent

100 Miles

100 Kilometers

Islamic World

632 Muhammad dies in Medina

632–634 Abu Bakr is first caliph; gains control over all of Arabia

634–644 Umar is second caliph; governs new Muslim lands in Syria, Egypt, and Persia

644 Umar forms first council

644–656 Uthman is third caliph; Quran is written down for the first time

660 Shurta police force established

656–661 Ali is fourth caliph

685–705 Abd al-Malik makes Arabic the official language

700s Structured system of Sharia law develops

700s Hanafi and Maliki schools of law develop

750–800 Peak of Abbasid power; role of vizier or chief advisor created

800s Shafii, Hanbali, and Jafari schools of law well established

945 Buyids take over the Abbasid capital of Baghdad

1055–1258 Abbasid authority declines

1055 Seljuk Turks defeat the Buyids and gain control of Baghdad

1099 Crusaders attack Jerusalem

1187 Saladin regains control of Jerusalem

1258 Mongols attack Baghdad, killing the Abbasid caliph

1281 Ottoman Empire founded in Turkey

1520–1566 Suleiman develops a new legal system

1923 In Turkey, last Ottoman sultan replaced by a president

Rest of the World

700s Feudal system of lords and serfs, or servants, is established in Europe

768 Under the European ruler Charlemagne, local counts rule different regions

871 King Alfred codifies English law

1045–1085 Isaac Alfasi writes about practical law in the Talmud, or Jewish Scriptures

1066 William I brings the feudal system to England

1100 Henry I of England creates a system of representatives who administer justice

1122 Canon, or church, law evolves; the pope is given legal authority in certain cases

1125 German princes decree new rulers will be elected

1164 Henry II of England develops a strong new government

1215 England's King John signs the Magna Carta, reducing the king's absolute power

1215 Pope Innocent III denounces using duels or ordeals to judge guilt

1295 A model parliament is created in England

1358 French lower classes revolt, hoping to reform the government

1381 English peasants rebel against a new tax

1531 Italian Andrea Alciato publishes a major work on civil law

Glossary

Allah The one true God of Islam; from *al* (the) *ilah* (god)

allies People who fight on the same side

Bedouin Nomadic person of the Middle Eastern deserts

caliphs Muslim leaders after Muhammad

caliphate Area controlled by the caliph

caravan A group of people and animals traveling together, usually carrying trade goods, often across a desert

civil wars Conflicts between citizens, or ordinary people, living in a country

council A group of people who together settle an issue

dynasty Series of rulers from one family

elders Older, wiser members of a community

emirs Muslim military leaders or chiefs

fatwa A ruling on a point of Islamic law

Fiqh The study of Islamic law

firman A decree made by a Muslim ruler

ghilmans Prisoners that Muslims trained to be slave soldiers

government The group of officials who look after a country and its people

governors Officials whose job is to look after a region

hadiths The collection of words and actions of Muhammad

harem Part of a Muslim household specifically for women to live in

imam Muslim religious teacher or leader

independent Free from outside control

Islam The religion or faith based on God's messages to Muhammad

Janissary Corps Royal bodyguards and soldiers of the Ottoman Empire

Kaaba The holiest site in Islam, a square building in Mecca

mosque Muslim house of worship

mufti A Muslim legal expert

Muslim A person who follows the faith of Islam

nomads People with no fixed home, who instead move from place to place

oases A fertile patch in the desert

peninsula Area of land projecting into the sea

prophet A religious teacher who was inspired by God, as Muhammad was

qadi A Muslim judge

Quran Islam's holy book, containing the messages Muhammad said came from God

recitation Something told from memory

republic A state in which people elect their leaders

scribes People who write things down

secular Things of the world, rather than of God or religion

Sharia Muslim guidelines for laws

Shii Believers in leadership of Muslims based on family links to Muhammad

shurta Police in the early Islamic Empire

sultan A Muslim ruler

Sunni Believers in leadership of Muslims based on choice of the umma

ulema Religious scholars

umma Community of Muslims

vizier An advisor to a Muslim ruler

Further Information

Books

Davis, Lucile. *Life During the Great Civilizations: The Ottoman Empire.* San Diego: Blackbirch Press, 2004.

Greenblatt, Miriam. *Süleyman the Magnificent and the Ottoman Empire* (Great Explorations Benchmark). Singapore: Marshall Cavendish, 2002.

Grieve, Paul. *A Brief Guide to Islam: History, Faith and Politics: The Complete Introduction.* New York: Carroll and Graf, 2006.

Mantin, Peter, and Ruth Mantin. *The Islamic World: Beliefs and Civilizations.* Cambridge, England: Cambridge University Press, 1993.

Spilsbury, Louise, and Richard Spilsbury. *The Islamic Empires* (Time Travel Guide). Mankato, MN: Heinemann-Raintree, 2007.

Websites

Islamic Civilization
**www.factmonster.com/dk/encyclopedia/
islamic-civilization.html**

Islam Primer: The Islamic World—History, Beliefs, and Culture
www.factmonster.com/spot/islam.html

PBS—Islam: Empire of Faith
www.pbs.org/empires/islam

Islam
www.kidspast.com/world-history/0171-islam.php

Video

Islam: Empire of Faith. PBS Documentary, 2005.

Index